Champions

Helen Chapman

Editorial consultants:
Cliff Moon and Lorraine Petersen

D0184195

RISING★STARS

Close,

London W1S 4EX
www.risingstars-uk.com

Published 2007

Cover design: Button plc
Illustrator: Patrick Boyer
Text design and typesetting: Andy Wilson
Publisher: Gill Budgell
Commissioning editor: Catherine Baker
Publishing manager: Lesley Densham
Editor: Clare Robertson
Editorial consultants: Cliff Moon and Lorraine Petersen

British Library Cataloguing in Publication Data.
A CIP record for this book is available from the British Library

ISBN: 978-1-84680-205-8

Printed by Craft Print International Limited, Singapore

Contents

Characters

Harry He's new to BMX, but learning fast.

Kylie Harry's best friend, and a newbie too.

Ace The best BMX rider. He's not keen on Harry.

Agro Agro's good, but not as good as Ace.

Bazza Bazza is mates with Agro and Ace.

The Narrator The Narrator tells the story.

Scene 1
BMX v boarders

Narrator Ace, Bazza and Agro are BMX mad.
They put up with new riders Harry
and Kylie. But they don't put up
with skateboarders. They hate them.

Harry The park is packed today.

Ace It's all the skateboarders.
They're everywhere.

Agro It's hard to ride.

Bazza They think they own the park.

Harry They're always in our way.

Kylie They have a right to be here too.

Ace   No they don't!

Bazza   It's not just the park.

Agro   They're on the street.

Harry   And in the car park.

Kylie   Why don't you share?

Narrator   Ace, Bazza and Agro crack up laughing.

Ace   What?

Bazza   Why should we?

Agro   You are such a girl.

Kylie   Well, duh!

Harry   What's the point of riding our bikes if we can't do anything?

Agro   He's right. If we can't do tricks we may as well go home.

Bazza   Skateboarders think they rule
the park.

Kylie   They do!

Ace   Not any more.
I'll show them who's boss!

Agro   Go on. Make them show us respect.

Narrator   Ace rides into the skateboarders.
He pulls his bike into a standing
nose wheelie.

Kylie   Even I can do that, Ace. Big deal!

Ace   Bet you can't do this.

Kylie   What's he doing?

Bazza   Looks like the Kiss of Death.

Kylie   Looks like the Idiot Shows Off
if you ask me.

Agro   But we didn't ask you, Kylie.

Ace   Hey, are you watching?

Narrator   The back tyre rises. Ace bends
his knees and lets the back
of the bike lift up under him until
the seat almost hits his butt.

Harry   Wow! Way to go Ace.

Bazza   He's okay. Anyone can do
the Kiss of Death.

Agro   Yeah, if your front brakes are good.

Harry   Mine are good, but I still can't
do what he's doing.

Kylie   And I don't want to. I'll stick
with bunny hops.

Ace   Hey Kylie, do you want a kiss?

Kylie   I'll give it a miss thanks Ace.

Ace   Watch what you're missing then.

Kylie   What is he on about?

Bazza   Just watch him.

Narrator   Ace leans forward really far.
He tucks his head between his legs
and smacks a sloppy kiss on the seat
before the bike goes back down.

Harry   Ace! Watch out!

Narrator   Skateboarders do wheelies
around Ace's bike.

Agro   Get lost, you morons.

Bazza   Clear off.

Narrator Ace slams on the brakes so that
he won't hit the skateboarders.

Harry Are you all right?

Ace I'm sweet, but I so wanted to run
them down.

Agro Why didn't you?

Bazza They're laughing at us now!
And it's because of you, Ace.

Kylie Come on Ace, what are you
going to do?

Ace I don't know!

Harry You should, you're the best BMX
rider here.

Bazza Well, that's what he keeps telling us.

Harry I have a brainwave.

Ace That would be a first.

Agro Yeah, didn't know you had a brain.

Narrator   Harry ignores Ace and Agro.
He knows they will laugh down
anything he says.

Harry   We don't have a proper BMX
park, right?

Bazza   Other towns do.

Kylie   But we're not in another town,
are we?

Agro   We would be if we weren't
in this one.

Ace   I wish you guys *were* in
another town.

Harry   So, why not make our own?

Bazza   Own what?

Harry   BMX park.

Ace   That's stupid.

Bazza   We can't.

Harry   Why not?

Agro   Because we don't know how to.

Kylie   And where would we put it?

Narrator   Harry points to the picnic area.
No one eats there now because
the skateboarders are more
of a pest than the ants.

Kylie   I guess we can add stuff to
the tables and benches.

Agro   I get you! And make it good
for BMX bikes.

Bazza   And bad for skateboarders.
               Good one, mate.

Harry   The war is on!
               Those skateboarders are history.

Narrator But now Ace thinks Harry
               is trying to take over.
               If Ace has his way it will
               be Harry who is history.

Scene 2
A junk yard dog

Narrator They set off for the junk yard.
Ace lags behind. What makes Harry
think he can show him up?
He has to put him in his place.

Kylie This is so cool, you know.

Harry I know! Those three have never
listened to me before.

Kylie It's about time Ace sees that
he can't boss everyone all the time.

Narrator Ace needs to know what Agro
and Bazza think.

Ace   Hey, Agro, Bazza, slow down.

Agro   No, you catch up.

Bazza   What's Ace's problem?

Agro   Don't know, but we have the street to ourselves so I'm not slowing down.

Narrator   Ace speeds up and pulls up by his friends.

Ace   I don't get it, guys. Why are you listening to Harry and not me?

Agro   It's no big deal.

Bazza   And anyway, Harry's come up with a brainwave. Got a better idea?

Ace   Plenty.

Agro   Don't sweat it, Ace. You're still
the best BMX rider we've got.
Everyone knows that.
Harry too.

Ace   It doesn't feel like it.

Bazza   Poor diddums – is wimpy Harry
getting you upset?

Narrator   Up ahead, Harry and Kylie
cross an empty block of land.
They turn into Jim's junk yard.
Harry sees the boys speeding past.

Harry   Oi, you lot. Over here!

Narrator   They race into the driveway.
Agro and Bazza get off their bikes.
Ace doesn't.

Kylie   Where do we start?

Harry   Look for anything we can use
as a ramp.

Agro   But a ramp has to go against
          something.

Harry We've got the picnic tables,
          the benches and the barbeques.

Bazza There's heaps of stuff here.

Kylie Hey, there's a door! It'd make
          a cool ramp.

Harry We need stuff that's easy
          to take back.

Bazza Me and Agro can carry that.

Kylie This looks good.

Agro   And this.

Scene 2   A junk yard dog

Narrator A dog comes up to Harry
and sniffs his backpack.

Harry Hello fella, you hungry?
Let's see what I can find.

Ace I'm sick of hanging around.
I'll see you back at the park.

Bazza Wait up mate, we need
your help to carry stuff.

Kylie I'll go and see how much
this stuff will cost.

Ace You mean we have to pay?
Some brainwave this is.

Narrator On the ride back, the BMX riders
look like circus riders. Harry and
Kylie each hold a piece of timber
with one hand. They hold the bar
with the other hand.

Harry Are you all right? You're wobbling.

Kylie   I'm fine if I don't look back.

Harry   Here's an idea, don't look back.

Kylie   I can't help it. That dog from
the junk yard is following you.

Bazza   Harry, that dog thinks you rock.

Ace   Whose side are you on?

Bazza   Ah, come on Ace, I'm just being
friendly.

Ace   With that little no-mates?

Harry   If the dog stays I'll take her back on
my way home.

Agro   She can be our mascot.

Kylie   You three are way cool.
You look like stunt riders.

Bazza   We are, sort of.

Agro   Riding with no hands is easy.

Harry   But you're all holding a big plank
of timber between your bikes.

Kylie   I could never do that.

Harry   Nor me.

Narrator   Ace slows down. He has had an idea.
A way to get back at Harry.
All he has to do is get Agro
and Bazza on his side.
Then nothing will go wrong.
He starts to work on his plan.

Ace   You're such a loser, Harry.
Kylie's a girl but you have no excuse.
Hey Agro, do you know anyone else
who can ride like us?

Agro   Nah!

Bazza   We're the best. You want to be
as good as us? Watch and learn, kids,
watch and learn.

Scene 3
The contest

Narrator Back at the park, the BMX
riders get off their bikes.
They lay them on the ground
and take their helmets off.
Together they drag the planks
up to the picnic tables.

Kylie It all looks a bit wonky. Is it safe?

Harry Er … it doesn't look safe, does it?

Narrator Ace sees his chance to start
his plan. He whispers something
to Agro and Bazza. Then he stares
at Harry.

Ace   Who wants safe?

Narrator Ace waits but no one says anything.
Then Ace hits Agro to get him
to say something.

Agro   Yeah, safe is for losers.

Bazza   We want danger.

Kylie   Fine. Who wants to go first then?

Harry   Me! It was my idea, so I should
be first.

Ace   No chance! I'm the best rider.
I always go first.

Narrator Ace winks at Agro.

Agro   And I always go second.

Bazza   That's how it's always been.

Harry   That doesn't mean it has to stay
that way.

Ace Yes it does. I'm going first.

Kylie Last time you went first, all you
did was give the skateboarders
a good laugh.

Ace That could have happened
to anybody.

Harry But it didn't! It happened to you.

Ace I want this sorted.
We'll have a contest.
The best rider gets free drinks later.
Oh, and everyone has to do
what they say. For the rest
of the day.

Agro Cool!

Bazza Seems fair to me.

Kylie No it isn't! Harry's a newbie.

Harry There's no way I can win.

Ace   Tough luck, loser.
        You started it.

Bazza   Now you've got to end it.

Agro   Yeah, you don't mess with Ace.

Kylie   But you can't have a contest!
         Harry's a new rider and you're
         really good.

Ace   I tell you what.
        I'll help you out.
        We can do the contest as a team.

Kylie   What? Have one side against
         the other?

Ace   Why not? So go on Harry, pick
        the rider you want.

Harry   I don't trust you, you're
         up to something.

Narrator Ace *is* up to something. He knows
he can't lose. If Harry picks Agro,
Ace will tell Agro to mess up.
And if Harry picks Bazza,
Ace will tell Bazza to mess up.

Ace No I'm not! I just want to give you
a sporting chance.

Bazza Mate, to do that you'll have to ride
with your eyes shut.

Agro Yeah, and with no hands.

Harry I'll have Kylie.

Ace What?

Harry I said I'll have Kylie.

Ace Why?

Harry She's my best mate.

Narrator Ace drags his friends into a huddle.

Agro Now what do we do?

Ace You still need to make sure I win.

Bazza How can you lose?

Agro Yeah, against those two.

Narrator Ace, Agro and Bazza walk around the picnic area. They are whispering to each other. Harry and Kylie put their helmets on.

Bazza I think each rider should get one practice run.

Harry Good idea.

Kylie Fine by me.

Narrator   Ace, Bazza and Agro just want
to see how best to mess up
Harry's and Kylie's tricks.

Harry   What are you best at, Kylie?

Kylie   I can ride my bike facing backwards.

Harry   Can you do that up the ramp?

Narrator   The dog runs up and down the ramp.

Kylie   Not with the dog there.

Harry   Oi, girl. Come here.

Narrator   Harry puts the dog by the rest
of the bikes and helmets.

Bazza   She looks like a guard dog.

Narrator Kylie wants to do a harder trick.
She rides on to the picnic table
and grabs the bike seat. She pulls
up and gets the front wheel off
the table. She spins the handlebars
twice and jumps the bike down
onto the ground.

Harry Wow! That was great!

Ace What trick are you doing Harry?

Agro Apart from trying to stay on.

Harry This!

Narrator Harry rides up the ramp and along
the picnic table. He goes off
the ramp at the other end
and lands with his back tyre first.

Kylie Well done!

Scene 3   The contest

Narrator Ace turns to his friends.

Ace   You guys are right.
               There's no way I can lose.

Scene 4
Who let
the dog out?

Narrator Harry and Kylie are excited
because they did well. Ace is happy
because he's about to show off.

Ace Agro, get your helmet.
You're on my team.

Bazza What about me?

Agro What about you?

Ace Agro is heaps better than you.

Kylie Bazza, you can say who does
the best trick.

Bazza   You trust me?

Harry   Yes. You know how hard the tricks are.

Kylie   And you can tell if we do them
the right way.

Bazza   Okay.

Narrator   Ace and Agro walk to their bikes.
Ace gives a shout.

Ace   My tyre! It's wrecked.

Agro   Let me see.

Bazza   Skateboarders did this.

Kylie   They can't have.
We'd have seen them.

Agro   It looks chewed, but how …?

Harry   Um … I think the dog's done it.

Ace   You put it by the bikes.
It's your fault.

Kylie   It's a dog! Dogs chew things.
Live with it.

Bazza   You can use my bike.

Narrator Agro picks up his helmet.

Agro   Phew! What's that stink?
Gross! It's wet!
That dog's out to get us.

Bazza   You can use my helmet.

Agro   Nah, you might have nits.
I once got nits from wearing
another kid's helmet.

Harry   That's too much information.

Agro   I won't ride without a helmet.

Ace   Sweet, I'll go it alone.
I'll do the Superman.
It'll blow you guys away.

Kylie   The Superman?

Bazza   He named it after himself.

Kylie   He would!

Narrator   Ace races the bike up the ramp.
The dog runs after him.
Ace jumps the bike up
on to the picnic table.

Bazza   Mate, don't speed up.

Narrator   It's too late for Ace to stop.
The dog leaps at his chest.
Ace grabs the dog. Ace and
the dog and the bike fall
to the ground.

Harry   Wow! We've got Superman
and his Superdog.

Kylie   Ace, you're such a star!
You stopped doing your trick
so that you wouldn't hurt
the dog.

Agro   It's no big deal.
             He fell on his head.

Narrator Ace takes off his helmet
              and rubs his head.

Ace   And that's why we wear
             a brain-bucket, kiddies.

Agro   Yeah, but it's so sad that
             you don't have a brain
             to put in it.

Ace   That's so funny I forgot to laugh.
             Can one of you guys get this dog
             off me?

Narrator As Harry grabs at the dog
it runs off barking. Harry and Kylie
run after it. They are stopped
by a woman.

Bazza Who's that with Harry and Kylie?

Agro It's a park ranger.
She's looking at the ramps
and shaking her head.

Ace Now she's looking at the dog
and shaking her head.

Narrator Harry, Kylie and the dog
walk back to the others.

Ace Thanks to that stupid dog
I've lost the contest.

Harry We've lost more than that.
The park ranger said the ramps
have to go.

Kylie   And we can't ride here any more.
She said we could ride into people.

Agro   How did she find us?
The picnic area has trees around it.

Harry   She heard the dog barking.
Dogs aren't allowed.

Ace   Where can we ride?

Agro   Your brainwave's made things worse.

Harry   I know. Look, I'll take the dog
back to the junk yard.

Kylie   I'll come too.

Narrator   They stop as a man comes
up to them. He takes the dog
and Harry and Kylie hurry back.

Ace   Who was that?

Kylie   Jim from the junk yard.
He thanked Harry for finding
his lost dog.

Bazza   Thanked him! It was because of
Harry that the dog went missing.

Harry   We didn't tell him that bit.

Kylie   Harry told Jim that the dog
got us kicked out of the park.

Harry   Jim said that he can help.
He has an empty block of land
by the junk yard.

Kylie   And we can ride there.

Agro   Now?

Kylie   Any time we want to.

Bazza   What are we waiting for?
Lead on, Harry.

Harry   Ace should go first.

Ace   No, I lost the contest.

Harry   Only because you did the right
thing and saved the dog
from being hurt. Let's see if Jim
has a spare tyre, then we'll
check out our new BMX park.

Narrator   They ride off to spend the rest
of the day at the new park.
With not a single skateboarder
to be seen.

Drama ideas

After Scene 1

- Hotseating: choose one person to be Ace.
- Everyone else can ask Ace questions, e.g. what does he think about Harry, and why? What is he planning to do next?

After Scene 2

- With a partner, pretend to be Ace and Harry.
- Ace should think of reasons why Harry's idea of the BMX park is a bad one. Harry should think of reasons why it is a good idea.
- Have a pretend argument about it. Then decide – should they build the park?

After Scene 3

- In your group, decide what
  you think will happen next.
  Will Ace win the contest?
  Or will something else happen?
- Act out your ideas.

After Scene 4

- In your group, each choose
  a character from the play.
- Take on the role of your character
  and tell everyone else what
  happens to your character
  after the end of the play.